Hands On Plan

To Leann, Todd, & Cason

Thank you so much for your hospitality!!!

♡ Nancy 🙂

Hands On Plan

How to use Emotional Freedom Technique to
tap into a happy and successful life

Nancy Tilton Hand, JD

Create the life you want.

A Tilton Seminars Publication
© 2018 Nancy Tilton Hand
Print Edition
Nancy Tilton Hand, JD
Tilton Seminars, LLC
P.O. Box 3154 Auburn, AL 36831
www.nancytiltonhand.com
info@nancytiltonhand.com

Cover art and internal diagrams by Nancy Tilton Hand, JD. Back cover photo by Will Hand.

Hand, Nancy, T.
Hands On Plan
Bibliography
ISBN 13: 978-0-9837276-2-0 (E-Book)
ISBN 13: 978-0-9837276-3-7 (Paperback) – Library of Congress Control Number: 2016919514
1. Motivation 2. Stress Management 3. Information Management 4. Overwhelm 5. NLP 6. EFT

For Will.

Where there is a Will, there is a way.
I could not have done this without you!

Contents

Introduction

Do you have a master plan for your life? If you have one, how effective is it? Are things running smoothly? Do things work out the way you want them to most of the time? Are you happy?

It is so easy to get caught up in life and push planning to the side. Have you ever thought about doing something more with your plan but never had the time?

What if you took the time to do it?

I did, and it changed my life – for good.

In fact, the quality of my life has improved in ways I never could have imagined. It started small with wishes and hopes jotted down on notepads and on the backs of receipts. Over time, it evolved into the Hands On Plan.

The Hands On Plan is a process and a system that I use constantly. It has had such a profound effect on my life that I finally decided to write it down so that you can apply the formula to your life, too.

My plans work out the way I want them to. My ideal outcomes come to fruition consistently and easily. Sometimes things happen differently than I expect them to, but the end result is almost always what I wanted it to be.

How would you like to get the same results?

Lucky for you, I have had over 16 years to perfect and polish this process. Now it is distilled into an intuitive formula that you can apply right away.

With practice, it will come to you naturally. You will begin to use the Hands On Plan easily and automatically. You will not even have to think about it.

You will notice that life just works better. It is also a lot more fun!

It all started with the bar exam…

I wanted to pass the bar exam so badly that I applied every possible advantage (see my first book, "Beyond Rainmaking"). The Louisiana Bar Exam is a notoriously difficult exam. After hearing many scary stories, I wanted to be sure that I was prepared (and then some).

I started to write my plans in a journal. That enabled me to relax and study more effectively. The clearer my focus and purpose became, the more confident I felt.

Other parts of my life began to fall in line with my goal. Everything I did supported my ideal outcome of passing the bar exam the first time. That translated into less time studying and extra time to do things like work out, walk the dog, and work on my photography.

The Hands On Plan was born.

The bar exam study time is one of my favorite memories. I actually enjoyed it! It was a great time in my life.

Having that internal plan and direction made all the difference in my attitude. I passed the bar exam easily the first time. I even skipped a section (a practice that is heartily discouraged)!

Since then, the Hands On Plan (HOP) has been constantly improved and adjusted. It has been pared down and distilled into a *powerful* tool for identifying and getting what you want.

No matter what your project, the HOP produces consistent, reliable results. I want you to have the results you want so that your life is exactly the way you want it to be – YOUR ideal outcomes realized.

Why now?

When I was writing my own HOP this year, I reviewed the one from last year. It was a phenomenal year! So was the one before that and the one before that. Every year the results of my HOP turn out better than the year before.

Better. Every. Year.

It dawned on me that this plan is something special. It has been a game changer for me. It is time for me to share it with you.

Here are some things you need to know about this process.

It works!

That might feel weird at first, especially if you are not accustomed to things working out the way you want them to. It might feel strange or selfish to focus on your desires. You might be unnerved at the difference you can make in your life using this technique.

You *will* get used to it!

Oh yes, you will get used to things working out. You will begin to expect things to come together and support you. You will get used to feeling good, having the money you want, and enjoying life.

That is why we are here, right?

It works for you even when you do not work it.

(See my special note at the end of this book)

The HOP works amazingly well when you work it. It still works when you do it half-heartedly. There have been many times when I revisited old notebooks to find a hastily sketched out purpose or desire that had already come into my life.

It works when you feel like you have no real control over the situation.

The HOP even works in times when nature, traffic, or a difficult person could sabotage your beneficial outcome.

It still works when you do it at the very last minute.

You can jot your HOP down hours or even minutes before you need it and it will still help!

Let me tell you about the dance floor…

My husband and I had a magical wedding on the beach at a gorgeous bed and breakfast. Things went amazingly well – almost too well!

Then out of the blue something happened that threatened to derail the whole shebang. I mean, it was a wedding, right? Something had to happen. It is tradition!

The dance floor arrived on Thursday afternoon for our Saturday evening wedding. When the vendors began assembling it on the lawn, the bed and breakfast manager said, "No way!" and tried to get them to take the floor up.

She called me over and over screaming that we were going to ruin the lawn and that we had to remove the floor. I was split between trying to deal with her and convincing the floor rental guys to leave the dance floor on the lawn.

My calmness crumbled. I was more than a little upset. I was mad!

My husband-to-be was already well versed in the HOP. He looked at me and asked, "What do you want?"

He was so right! We sat down together and wrote out our best-case scenario. It was short and sweet.

We wanted the bed and breakfast manager to just go away. Maybe she could be completely distracted by something else and forget about us?

The result was immediate and amazing. The phone calls stopped. The manager left the floor vendor alone. She just disappeared!

She was not even there on the day of our wedding. She just disappeared and left us alone. The lawn, by the way, survived and thrives to this day.

I have many more stories. Stories of vacations that went smoothly and were magical. Stories of tests that were easily passed. Stories of being in the right place at the right time (and meeting the right people). All of these possibilities become much more likely when you know what you want.

And then there is the flip side…

Here are some great indicators that you do *not* have an HOP:

- ***Difficulty making a decision.*** You might go down to the wire trying to decide what to do because things are not clear enough. That can lead to...

- ***Missed opportunities and regret.*** No HOP means no benchmark for your decision. No coordinates. You might not recognize a great opportunity until it is too late.

- ***Awkward. Adrift. Off-balance.*** Not having an HOP leaves you off-kilter, unbalanced, and subject to other people's control.

- ***Drama.*** Without a clear HOP, you are much more likely to end up embroiled in other people's business, taking on too much responsibility, or in situations that lead you astray.

When you have a plan and know the steps, it is easier to say "no" when you need to. You recognize and dodge drama before it is too late. Instead of being drawn off course, you stay focused and make rapid progress.

Learn and use the HOP so that you can live an amazing life full of joy. You will get used to telling fascinating stories about things that worked out right.

One more thing before we get into the plan...

It may not seem like it, but I am a total skeptic. I need to know how things work.

Are you like me? Do you need proof, too?

I thought you might. That is why I made sure to show you some of the scientific research that supports every step of this process.

The first chapter is an explanation of why this plan works so well. In the rest of the chapters, we will talk about how to use the techniques to put together your own HOP.

I will give you the latest, most up-to-date version of my formula so that you can create a joyful, successful, and prosperous future. You can immediately start creating the life you have always wanted.

Before you get started…

Think about the year to come (from today to this day next year). How would you rate your hope, enthusiasm, and confidence about having a great year on a scale of 1-10 (with 10 being high)?

Using that same scale, where would you rate your fear, stress, or worry about things to come?

Make a note of these numbers right now. This is your baseline. By the end of this book, those numbers will be radically different!

CHAPTER 1

Step 1

Write Now

"The pen is mightier than the sword."
~Edward Bulwer-Lytton

Writing out your best-case scenario is mighty powerful!

The magic of the HOP is that it aligns you with your written best-case scenario. It does not matter where or how you write it – on a computer, in a journal, on the back of a napkin. Writing it down changes everything.

Own your desires

When you write down your best-case scenario it becomes real. Tangible.

It brings your desire into clear focus. It validates your ideal outcome. Knowing your ideal outcome can reveal the true reason or purpose behind your desire – your WHY.

Recognizing your desires honestly also gives you an opportunity to manage any fear or doubt that may arise regarding achieving your ideal outcome. It will help you create a clear route to obtaining the object of your desire.

Empower your plans

Writing down your best-case scenario gives it power and empowers you to achieve it. Get the WHY right and even a haphazard plan can pay off.

Have you ever been *all in*? When you are 100% behind your goal, even a shoddy, poorly implemented plan can produce reasonably good results.

You have already experienced times in your life when the planets seemed to align for you to get what you wanted. Things came together to support your success in wonderfully unexpected ways. *It was because you were aligned with your purpose – your why.*

No WHY? No HOW!

The opposite is also true. How many times have you created detailed plans only to have them fall apart or go off course? Unless you are aligned with your purpose (your *why*) the plans you make (your *how*) will be difficult to manage.

Turn dreams into reality

Writing down your best-case scenario brings it to life.

Have you ever noticed that the plans you keep in your head tend to stay there? That is because writing them down is the step between dream and reality (just like blueprints are for a building).

The emotional impact of writing down your best-case scenario is powerful. You affirm your goal in the real world. That affirmation acts as a compass to keep you on track toward your desired outcome.[1]

Save time and money

You may have heard that planning has the highest rate of return of any other business activity. It helps you to maximize resources, build in safeguards, and better predict outcomes. This is just as true for your personal life as it is for business.

Write down your best-case scenario so that you can save time and money by easily:

- Focusing on your goal
- Making timely decisions
- Streamlining activities
- Avoiding unnecessary expenses
- Spotting opportunity

Navigate to success

Your written best-case scenario acts like a beacon. It draws you toward the goal. You become clear about your desire and congruent with it.

Congruence is an incredibly powerful influencer. When you are congruent, everything you say and do lines up to support your success. You easily maintain control over outside influences.

Your momentum and enthusiasm attract cooperative and helpful people to you. Who can resist a person with a clear purpose?

Be smarter

Did you know that having a written best-case scenario clears your working memory?

Writing down your defined purpose can clear your working memory, making you more mentally nimble. It makes it easier for you to learn and process new information.

When you keep plans in your head, they take up room in your working memory. The information bounces around in your brain like a bunch of lottery balls. It leaves little room for creative thinking, recall, and higher functioning.

Instead of uplifting and motivating you, your goal becomes a source of stress and anxiety. Even worse, the anxiety can steer you into hasty decisions, guessing, procrastination, and half-hearted work.

Free your working memory! Writing down best-case scenarios for your goals gets them out of your head and onto the page. It gives you the mental space to be resourceful.

You will be able to process information faster, learn more, retain more of what you learn, and recall it when you want it. You will file new information into your long-term memory more efficiently so that recall is effortless and accurate.

Get motivated

Your written best-case scenario will pull you toward your goal like a magnet. You will *want* to work on it. Pursuing your goal will be *fun* and satisfying even when it is challenging.

You will more easily and enthusiastically make changes to your lifestyle that support your success. Knowing your desired outcome gives you a motivating purpose for making positive changes.

Filter out distractions and negativity

Your written best-case scenario acts as a powerful filtration system. Once you know what you want, you have an easier time avoiding pitfalls of all kinds.

A written best-case scenario keeps your mind from constantly wandering to the worst possible outcome. This is one of the most compelling reasons to write down your ideal outcome. It trains your brain to focus on the goal instead of the "what ifs."

It will also help you to naturally avoid people and situations that might deter you from your goal or throw you off course. It can be easy for other people to throw you off track. Having the destination clearly in mind will keep that from happening to you.

When you make the decision to focus on your best-case scenario, some parts of your life might shift. Situations will change. Relationships might naturally adjust or dissolve.

It may even be uncomfortable in the moment. Trust that it means new and better relationships are coming – ones that will support your success.

Enhance your insight

Having a written best-case scenario tunes your intuition, gut feelings, and hunches. When your intuition is tuned, you notice when something supports your purpose and when it does not.

That awareness gives you the ability to easily recognize opportunities. It also helps you to connect with people who will support you as you pursue your goal. You will be able to notice those people and cultivate relationships without hesitation.

Bust through stress

Your written best-case scenario keeps your mind from wandering and dwelling on the other possibilities. Just the simple act of knowing what you want out of a situation calms the fear and doubt that can accompany pursuing a goal.

Taming the uncertainty and managing the worry brings your stress levels down substantially. Your ability to be creative and resourceful goes way up when your stress level goes down.

Save relationships

A written best-case scenario will help to lower your stress levels. When your stress level goes down, you have the space and mindset to tend to yourself and your relationships.

Better yet, the enthusiasm and purpose you feel will be contagious. Positive, motivated people will be drawn to you. The people around you will begin to pick up your enthusiasm and positive attitude.

Use HOP for everything

A written best-case scenario works for anything! Your goal does not have to be monumental to use this technique. Not by a long shot!

Even little things can spark desire, cause stress, or demand change. *If it matters, write a best-case scenario* so that you can relax and focus on getting what you want.

Now What?

You understand the power of writing down your best-case scenario. However, discovering what your best-case scenario is can be one of the trickiest parts.

Sometimes it can be hard to pinpoint what you want. That difficulty can lead to frustration and goal abandonment.

In the next chapter, you will learn the part of this process that will ease your way. You will discover how to design best-case scenarios that are consistent with your greatest past successes.

Chapter 1 recap:

Write down your goals so that you can...

Own them

Empower your plans

Turn dreams into reality

Save time and money

Navigate to success

Be smarter

Get motivated

Filter out distractions and negativity

Enhance your insight

Bust through stress

Save relationships

CHAPTER 2

Step 2

Appreciate

At the beginning of this year I heard a lot of people making comments like, "This year is going to be better," "I'm SO glad last year is over," and "Good riddance to last year!"

For people expressing those sentiments, last year might have been disappointing or overly challenging. It could not have been all bad. They must have had great days, too.

Still, their year was disappointing enough to prompt them to express it publicly. That says something.

In literature it might be considered foreshadowing. You can probably predict how their next year will end up based on their assessment of last year. The difference is in the focus.

Even a challenging or disappointing year is a great year!

Have you ever heard of the 80/20 rule, the Pareto principle? It states that 80% of the effects come from 20% of the causes.

Much of your life goes pretty well. Still, the small percentage that goes awry or disappoints tends to get the most attention.

We are hardwired to notice when things go wrong. It is a survival instinct. Unchecked, the small percentage of your experiences that seem negative or bad will dominate your thoughts. They will guide your decisions.

If you focus solely on what went wrong or the disappointments of last year, you will create future plans based on unsatisfactory past results. How do you think those plans will work out?

Do not let your perceived failures be the governing force behind your future decisions! It creates a future based on disappointment!

While it is certainly true that you learn from your mistakes, you also learn a lot from your successes. If you learn from one and not the other, you get an incomplete education!

You are likely well-versed in what did not go well last year. What will happen now if you focus on the larger percentage of your life that went well?

Say these phrases out loud:

"I'm going to do better this year."

"I'm going to top last year!"

Those two phrases seem to say the same thing but don't they feel different?

"I'm going to do better this year." says, "I'm going to try to improve because last year was disappointing." It implies that your experience of last year was somehow substandard or a failure.

"I am going to top last year!" sounds more like last year was pretty good. It may have been challenging. There may have been disappointments. There may have been room for improvement. But it was good overall.

In seeking to top last year, you recognize the wins and high points, too. It says, "Last year was all right. Look at what I was able to achieve last year despite the challenges! I wonder what I can do this year to top last year?"

Last year was great! When you own that, you are going to be able to ride that wave of enthusiasm into another fabulous year.

You are already on your way to topping last year!

TOP last year (Totally Outdo your Past)

This year, when my husband and I sat down to write our HOPs together, we decided to TOP last year. To do that we had to first identify what went right.

That meant reviewing last year for what worked, what went well, what made us feel proud, and what brought us joy.

It was weird at first. The big things stood out, like milestones we reached and things checked off of the bucket list. As we discussed those obvious things, something cool happened...

It was like opening the door to a secret treasure room.

More and more good things came to mind. We remembered things that were checked off the "to do" list that had lingered too long. We recognized unexpected accomplishments that arose out of our hobbies.

Then it snowballed. He made his list. I made my list.

We made a list of our mutual "wins" and accomplishments. It included improvements on the house, travel, great times with friends, and professional successes.

It was an amazing process! Things continued to come up over the next few days. So many came to mind that we started keeping a running list of wins from last year.

Confidence in our abilities bloomed as we reviewed the lists. Our combined outlook improved immeasurably.

It felt like we were being rewarded, patted on the back, and given credit for all of our hard work. We were. By us!

Pat yourself on the back!

Are you waiting for someone else to acknowledge your successes? Do you spend most of your time dwelling on your shortcomings?

If so, then it is time to revel in your many successes. How can other people recognize them if you cast them off as unimportant?

Appreciate your successes! Stop waiting for someone else's praise and pat on the back.

Do it yourself! That was one of the biggest take-aways from this exercise. The feeling of recognizing and validating your own successes is a heady thing! By the end of it, we were feeling euphoric!

Build on your successes!

When you recognize and validate the things that went well, you can create more experiences like them. Then you have something to TOP.

We are already well on our way to topping last year.

You can TOP last year!

In the coming year, there will be challenges. Your strength will be tested. You will have to show up. There will almost certainly be some hard work involved.

Some things might not live up to your expectations. You may wish you had done a better job or done something differently.

For every one of those times there will be other times when you own it and you rock it.

You *will* have an amazing next year. You will shine and be resourceful. You will have some magnificent successes and many thousands of smaller wins.

You have probably thought a lot about the things you wish you could change about last year. Chances are, you have thoroughly reviewed that material.

Now turn your focus to what went well – let's call it the 80% – and lavish it with attention!

What went right last year?

You had a lot of fun. You had great conversations. You won. You got great service. You ate some delicious food. You were supported. You supported others. You loved and were loved. You overcame things. You heard great music. You healed. You earned. You learned. You were pleasantly surprised. You had the right tools for the job. You laughed. You were grateful. You did good work. You thought of something creative. You figured something out. You experienced beauty. You were in the right place at the right time.

SO much went well.

Recognizing and appreciating the good is the only way to build on what worked.

Appreciating the successes of last year is like putting a pin in the map and validating where you are. Then you have the whole picture. You know what you would have done differently, and you have acknowledged what went well.

Give yourself some credit for a job well done.

Build your year on a platform of appreciation! Look back at your year (this day last year to today) and sift for what worked.

Start making a list of your successes from last year. Write them down. This works especially well if you go into detail. Make your stories juicy!

Once you begin recalling memories of past successes, more will come to mind. You will be adding to and adjusting your list as you go along.

A great habit to develop is keeping a daily or weekly journal of your successes. That way you will have a full account of how wonderful your year is as it is happening.

The categories used in the HOP are: health, wealth, relationships, adventure, and surroundings.

Count your blessings!

Go through these categories one by one and write down as many of your successes as you can. List whatever comes to mind as a success or a win. Be sure to list things that made you proud or happy. Even the small successes are worth recording because they add up!

Health (Physical)

Over the course of a year, physical health can go through many changes, like weight loss, weight gain, illness, injuries, healing, growing, and strengthening. You may go through high energy times and low energy times. You may have medical or dental interventions.

How was your year?

Remember to focus on the positive. Did you get stronger? Did you kick a habit? Did you take up a healthier lifestyle? Did you stay healthy? Did you heal?

Health (Mental)

Think about how you improved mentally and emotionally over the past year.

You probably overcame challenges in a way that made you proud. You may have handled an emotional situation or argument especially well. You may have learned something new.

How did you improve, evolve, and grow?

Did you learn to treat yourself better? Did you find a particularly rewarding way to give back to your community?

That last one was one of my successes from last year. I started taking photos of adoptable pets at our local shelter. Some of the members of my photography club joined me.

It has made a big difference! Great photos help the animals find homes. Volunteer photographers get to practice their passion. Win-wins are always a success!

What did you learn last year?

Did you read any good books? Did you pick up nuggets of wisdom or learn a new skill?

Think about classes you may have taken. Any seminars, conferences, or even documentaries added to your knowledge base. They count!

You can also acknowledge your ongoing efforts to master a skill, like practicing yoga, playing the trumpet, or learning another language.

I spent a lot of time last year learning how to make sourdough bread. The process was fun, sometimes frustrating, and usually pretty tasty. Baking also helps me to feel balanced.

When did you feel truly grounded, connected, and balanced?

Were there times when you thought that things seemed to unfold perfectly?

You may have had moments of such pure beauty and joy that it took your breath away.

We kayak on a river near where we live. Every time we do it, there are moments when I just look around in awe and love. Wouldn't it be amazing to feel like that all of the time?

Wealth

Wealth comes in many shapes and sizes. In this category I tend to focus on financial wealth.

What gained value? Did your business or income grow? Did you get any especially good deals, savings, or bargains? Did you win anything? Did you make good investments? Did you get gifts or opportunities that felt like a treat?

Let me give you an example of what I mean by treat.

Last year we had the amazing fortune to go on three beach trips. One was our annual anniversary trip. We unplug, unwind, and work on our HOP. We think, journal, draw, read, and spend hours walking on the beach.

The second was with a group of friends, one of whom owns a beach house. Everybody chipped in to cover expenses and we spent a fantastic week at the beach playing games and enjoying life. What a treat!

The third was an annual family beach trip hosted by a family member. We contributed food and beverages, split kitchen duties, and had a wonderful beach week with family. Again, an amazing treat!

The trips with family and friends were absolutely relationship wins (quality time!) and health wins (stress relief!). They were also wealth wins.

Three weeks of beach is a lot of travel! Because of the way it worked out, we were able to enjoy those extraordinary trips and stay within our budget.

What about found or unexpected money?

We have a "found money" jar that is almost full. My best discovery last year was a paper dollar.

One year I found a one-hundred-dollar bill. Another year I found a (crushed)14K gold ruby ring kicked to the curb in a parking lot. Things like that count!

A few weeks ago, I received a check back to me for an overpayment. It was just over thirty dollars. It came out of the blue – unexpected and without obligation. That felt really good. Is that a financial win? Heck yes!

Who else loves a bargain? Those are wealth wins, too!

This past year, we stopped by an estate sale in our neighborhood and bought a brand new, $2000 vacuum cleaner (with all of the attachments and paperwork) for $15. That is certainly a wealth win!

What are your wealth wins for the year? Things appreciated. Money came in. You got deals and treats. You are going to be amazed when you start writing them down and adding them up!

Relationships

How were your relationships this past year? Who showed up to support you? Who did YOU show up to support?

Were you a good friend? Were your friends good to you?

Think back on your interactions from last year. You made some new relationships. Some of your existing relationships deepened and improved. Some may have run their course.

Write down the best things you can remember about your relationships and the people with whom you interacted. What were your best family or friend times? Who made you laugh the most?

On a special note…

After you go through this section, you might want to do something nice for the people who supported you. They are your best friends!

They may be waiting for a pat on the back and some recognition. Since they might not do it themselves, reach out and show them how much you appreciate them.

Adventure

This is one of my favorite sections because I love to travel. Of course, travel is not the only kind of adventure!

Throwing a party is an adventure. Hosting guests is an adventure. Graduations, babies, weddings, and holidays are all adventures. Even lunch or shopping with friends can be an adventure.

What were your adventures last year?

How were your holidays? Did you experience anything new? Did you check anything off of your bucket list? Did you have an especially good flight or other travel?

Think back on those times and write down your successes!

Surroundings

This can be a catch-all of the things in your life that underpin everything you do. Your house, car, pets, furniture, plants, wardrobe, and other "stuff" all fall into this category.

Did your car run well this year? Were the pets healthy? Did you get something fixed that had been on your mind for ages? Those are your successes.

What kind of success do I count in this area? We just had one!

Let me tell you about the conference table...

My father gave me a conference table when I started my law practice. It was 10' x 4'. It was a solid, beautiful, antique, English library table. It was a formidable piece of furniture.

After I moved to Alabama and changed careers, I no longer needed the table. I still loved it. Frankly it was a tough piece to sell for many reasons.

When I decided to sell it, I started asking around. Nobody wanted a table that big. Nobody wanted to spend that much money on a conference table.

I asked around for about a year. I listed it on a popular auction site. I *finally* decided to write an intention about it. My best-case scenario was for the table to go to the place where it would be appreciated and treated well.

Two days after writing my intention, I was on the phone with an attorney friend who has a small office here. I had considered offering it to him before but knew the table would be much too large for his office.

As we were ending the conversation, I asked if he might know someone who would be interested in a table like mine. Without missing a beat, he said he wanted to buy it. I sent pictures to him and he agreed to my asking price. Just like that.

Unbeknownst to me, he had recently finished restoring an office building in the historic district. He was having trouble finding furniture to fit the architecture. He said he could not find a table big enough to fit his conference room in the building. Mine was perfect.

Have you had something like that happen? If so, add it to your win list!

Chapter 2 recap:

Chapter 2 was all about validating and celebrating the things in your life that went well last year. They deserve your attention too!

We are trained as humans to focus on the few things that do not go right. The truth is, the vast majority of things do go right. If you only learn from your mistakes and not from your successes, you only get half of an education.

CHAPTER 3

Step 3

Tap into Your Success!

By now you probably have a great list of your successes and best experiences from last year. I bet they added up to more than you expected!

In recognizing and appreciating your successes, you have validated the 80% (or more) of your life that went well. You may be feeling much better about yourself and your experiences.

Want to take that to another level?

Introducing your new best friend: Tapping. It will enhance and increase the good feelings you have after making your success list. Use it to ingrain your successes and turbocharge your intentions for the future.

What is Tapping?

Tapping is also known as Emotional Freedom Technique (EFT), Meridian Tapping, and several other variations. It is the act of using your fingertips to tap certain points on the body in order to alleviate emotional stress. It is a way of altering emotions through touch intervention, thereby changing the resulting behavior.

Tapping is simple: you use your fingers to tap on certain points on the body while you think about your concern or objective. It calms the body and lowers stress levels.

The body-mind connection is well documented, especially when it comes to the effect of stress on the body. Stress is considered to be one of the top reasons for many mental and physical illnesses and is also a key factor in aging.

Tapping to relieve negative emotions is based on the theory that every behavior, pattern, or illness is a manifestation or representation of stored, stuffed, or un-dealt-with emotions that cause stress. Some of the emotions that commonly result from stress are sadness, trauma, regret, resentment, fear, and anger.

Tapping is an effective way to mitigate stress by diffusing the energy and negative emotions that cause it. Many of the Tapping points are the same as acupuncture and acupressure points.

That is the stock explanation.

Not good enough!

I want to know how and why something works.

When I first learned Tapping, nobody had a good explanation for how or why it worked. It worked (really well!) – but nobody could tell me specifically *how it worked.*

That information gap frustrated me. It also made it difficult for me to explain Tapping to other people. Simply saying, "It just works. It's like magic!" made me very uncomfortable.

I did my research. I cross-referenced. I deconstructed the process and did my best to figure it out.

I found out more than enough information to satisfy my logical brain. Tapping works incredibly well for many reasons.

If you are interested in finding out more about how it works, please look at Appendix A in the back of the book. If you are ready to start Tapping, here is how to do it.

How to Use Tapping

To tap, use your fingers to tap on the points shown on the diagram below. Tap gently but firmly. It should be comfortable. Be sure to cycle through the points.

Tapping Points

Tapping points are the same on both sides of the body. It does not matter which side you use.

If you are in public or cannot comfortably tap, you can hold the Tapping points and breathe deeply while you focus on the issue.

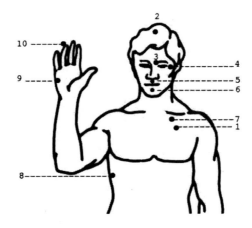

1. Sore spot

2. Top of head

3. Inside of eye

4. Outside of eye

5. Under nose

6. Chin

7. Collarbone

8. Under arm

9. Side of hand

10. Finger – at the inside edge of the nail bed

Tap in last year's successes

The best way to practice this part of the HOP process is by Tapping in stories of your success that are already written – by you.

Tap in all of those great memories and successes from last year. When you do, you will make those memories stronger and more vivid. You will also be setting yourself up for more success.

Here's to your success!

In the last chapter you learned how to recognize and document the wonderful things that have happened in your life over the past year. Use Tapping to turbo-charge, ingrain, and strengthen those great memories and "wins" from last year.

Did you know that you can improve confidence and performance in the present just by thinking about past successes?[2] Adding Tapping to the mix makes it work even better.

Get Tapping!

On your own body, gently tap on the points shown in the diagram while you recount (out loud, if possible) all of the wonderful things that happened in your life last year. Go category by category and savor feeling of accomplishment and appreciation.

Get into it! Be as detailed as you can. Let yourself re-experience those fabulous moments. You can enhance this exercise by recording it or dictating it into a document.

This is also a fun exercise to do with a good friend or partner *who is positive and supportive.* In fact, people who know you well might recognize some successes that you overlook. They may know when to ask you for more details or prompt you to go deeper into a memory so that your story is rich in detail.

You will feel uplifted and joyful while you are Tapping through the memories of past successes. If not, you might be feeling some resistance or those dastardly "yes, buts." Re-phrase your story until Tapping it out loud feels great. We will touch on how to tame the "yes, buts" in the next chapter.

After you have tapped in your past successes, you will be able to build on those successes. Your future will be designed in that mindset. You will more easily envision successful, fun, and satisfying outcomes for your goals.

Chapter 3 recap:

In chapter 3 you discovered how to use Emotional Freedom Technique (EFT). This is a wonderfully powerful combination of tried-and-true behavioral change techniques that you can use on your own. Try it on everything.

CHAPTER 4

Step 4

What Do You Want?

"Write down every single idea you have, no matter how big or small"
~Richard Branson

Now that you have tapped through everything that was great about last year, you probably feel wonderful. The next step, of course, is to turn toward the future.

Businesses have business plans. Architects have blueprints. High achievers *write down their goals*. Writing helps you zero in on what you want. It frees working memory so that you can devise creative solutions. It helps you hash out and manage resistance to the goal.[3]

Some of your goals may not merit a best-case scenario because you already feel assured of your success. Even so, it is good to acknowledge and validate the things that you think will go well.

For the important events, experiences, or predictable challenges, you will want to have a written best-case scenario.

How do you know what needs a best-case scenario?

I have to be straight with you here...this is the hard part.

If any part of this formula for an awesome life is tough to do, this is it. I usually set aside a chunk of time to do this part just to be done with it.

If you can do that, great! If it seems too stressful to do it all at once, go through the process sequentially starting with the least stressful category.

Work through it at an easy pace. Be sure to plan a treat, like a nice dinner, as a reward for your efforts.

Take as much time as you need. This is your plan!

You already know how to use the main categories (health, wealth, relationships, adventure, surroundings). Now look at each category individually and identify **predictable events** and **areas that require change**.

This is research. At this point, you are only identifying the issues for which you will write your best-case scenarios. You will be learning how to write them later on.

Identify predictable events

Unplanned things will certainly come up during the year. The best way to be prepared for those is to prepare for all of the predictable things ahead of time. Get them squared away in your mind so that your brain is available to manage new challenges as they arise.

Go category by category looking for predictable events.

Health

Predictable events in the health category can include everything from a fitness goal to check-ups to an upcoming dental appointment.

Wealth

The wealth category might include upcoming expenditures or investment opportunities. It could also include an upcoming work performance review or salary negotiation.

Relationships

Predictable events in the relationships category might include important conversations, networking opportunities, or mending fences with a loved one.

Adventure

The adventure category will most likely include holidays, travel, and life events. Weddings, birthdays, and graduations will be listed here. It can also include things like professional conferences or speaking engagements.

Surroundings

Predictable events in the surroundings category can include necessary wardrobe acquisitions for work or school (hard hat, suit, special shoes), home maintenance, car purchases, pet well-being, and landscaping.

The more predictable events you identify the better. If you think an important event might happen, go ahead and list it. You will be glad you did!

Identify areas that require change

Areas that require change are often your stressors. Listing all of your stressors can be overwhelming!

It's one thing to know they exist. It's another thing to label, acknowledge, and validate them. Still, you have to clearly know what they are before you can develop solutions for managing them.

Once you see all of your stressors laid out in front of you, you may feel a little bit better about your stress level. Many people feel like they are underperforming or slacking when nothing could be further from the truth.

You do a lot! The amount of stress you may be feeling is valid. By listing your stressors, you will be able to pinpoint the sources of stress and manage them in healthier ways.

Like before, go category by category and list the things that are bothering you, stressing you out, or causing you to worry. List all of your desires and needs.

It's ok if it seems trivial or if you feel awkward acknowledging your desires. Do it anyway. It will be helpful later.

If it seems like too much to do at one time, take it slowly and go category by category. You can always go back and change things. This is a working document meant to create focus, joy, and enthusiasm around your goals.

Health

Think about your health – your body and your mind. What are your fears, concerns, and expectations? Are there any appointments you have been putting off?

List everything you can think of as far as health stressors. List your wildest dreams in terms of health and well-being.

Are there things that you want to learn? List the things that would make you feel better about yourself.

Is there anything that you want to change? How do you want to look, feel, and be?

Wealth

What are your stressors in the wealth category? Maybe you have a big expense coming up or an opportunity to earn more money or invest. Maybe debt is weighing heavily on you. What keeps you up at night?

Write down your stressors and desired changes. Want to be debt free? Want a better income? Wish you had the extra income for travel? Write it down!

Relationships

Are any of your relationships causing you stress? You may have people in your life who drain your energy or drag you into drama.

Who do you send directly to voice mail? That might be a clue!

You might also want to grow your friend group and expand your sphere of influence. You may dream of going to great parties and meeting fascinating new people.

Or...you might WISH you wanted to meet new people but lack the desire or enthusiasm for it. It's ok. Write it down.

Adventure

Dreaming of doing things "someday?"

Want to run a marathon, go on vacation, or see your favorite performer live?

Maybe you would like a new travel companion or a workout buddy. Maybe you dream of skydiving or riding horses.

What adventures could you go on this year?

Surroundings

What about your surroundings? Think about the things that make your life run smoothly. Think about the systems that keep you going, like your house, office, and car.

Are you worried about any of them? If you have a house you may have a lot of stressors in this category.

Little stressors that add up – like a cabinet that does not close correctly. Things that linger too long on your "to do" list or that need to be fixed (…someday) can be sneakily stressful!

There is almost always something!

Once you have the things that need to be changed written down and identified, you can begin thinking about your best-case scenario for each of them.

Remember, no desire is frivolous! If it lights you up and pulls you forward, it is important.

Chapter 4 recap:

In chapter 4 you learned to sort things by predictable events and areas that require change – also known as stressors.

When looking into the future to create your best-case scenarios, go category by category listing predictable upcoming events and areas of your life that require change. You will know if an area requires change because it will probably be causing you stress.

CHAPTER 5

Step 5

When to Write a Best-case Scenario

"Things that matter most must never be at the mercy of things that matter least."
~Goethe

Now you have an exhaustive list of predictable upcoming events, things that are causing you stress, and desires. It may be overwhelming!

Relax, you will not need to make a best-case scenario for everything!

This next step will help you to **sift through and prioritize the important from the unimportant**. You will be able to easily sort everything on your list into manageable chunks.

Here is a method to help you sort for the things that DO need a best-case scenario:

Sort the items on your HOP based on "have to," "need," "want," and "would like."

For example…with a house, you *have to have* a functioning roof. You *need* a bathroom. You might *want* a paved driveway. You might *like* to have a great view, a comfortable sofa, a pool, or a deck.

Another way to determine the importance of an item (predictable event or area that requires change) is to rate it on a scale of 1-10, with 10 representing high and 1 representing low.

Here is a more detailed explanation:

Have to Have

Definitely write a best-case scenario!

When you *have to have* something, there is a lot riding on it. Not getting/becoming/doing that thing will result in dire consequences to your health, wealth, relationships, or reputation.

These are the make-or-break items. There is no plan B. It HAS to work out.

Something like this would likely be a 9 or 10 on your stress rating scale of 1-10. Being in the "have to have" mindset can cause a lot of stress! Recognizing this will help you to write a best-case scenario that opens up new possibilities.

Need

Definitely write a best-case scenario.

When you need something, it means that getting/becoming/doing that thing will substantially improve your circumstances. NOT getting/becoming/doing that thing would likely make your circumstances or path difficult, chaotic, or even impossible.

There may be a work-around, but it will not be fun or elegant.

You see this all of the time. Someone might *need* something, but they make do with what they have. What could they do if their need was fulfilled?

It would make life easier. It would relieve stress. It would move projects forward. It would improve efficiency. It might save money or time.

Want

Maybe write a best-case scenario.

Wanting something usually satisfies some desire and makes life easier and more fun. There may be something riding on it but probably nothing significant.

It is not that big of a deal. Life will go on if you do not become, do, or have that thing.

Writing a best-case scenario for something you want is your choice. How badly do you want it? How marvelous will things be if you get what you want?

Also, when you have a desire think about the future. What are the chances you will regret NOT getting / becoming/doing something you want?

Sometimes you have to use your imagination and think forward into the future.

Remember the Woodstock music festival? Yes, I mean that big, groundbreaking, not-to-be-missed concert in 1969 that shaped popular culture and a generation....

One of my mentors has an unbroken ticket to Woodstock. He really *wanted* to go. His mother said, "No."

He did not sneak out with his older friends and defy house rules. He was a good boy. He stayed home.

That's right. He MISSED WOODSTOCK.

He lived in New York City. The concert was right up the road...and he missed it.

He missed the mud, the wildness, and Jimi Hendrix playing the "The Star-Spangled Banner" as only Hendrix could do. He missed out on an iconic moment in history that shaped the world as we know it.

Of course, it can be hard to predict how something will turn out. Who knew that concert would forever change the face of music and our culture?

Still, how do you think he feels about that opportunity now?

I asked him if he could go back in time, would he have found a way to get there? Would he have broken the house rules?

YES! Woodstock would have clearly fallen into the HAVE TO category.

When deciding whether or not to write a best-case scenario for something you want, consider if you will ever have the chance again!

Even knowing this, my husband and I waivered when we had an opportunity to go to the Vienna Philharmonic New Year's concert. It was so expensive. We walked away from a tour guide who offered to sell us his extra tickets.

We walked a block or two before it hit us like a thousand "aha" moments. We stopped and looked at each other, "Whoa – what are we doing?!"

My mother and I listened to that concert together every year. We dreamed of someday hearing it live in the Golden Hall. It is almost impossible to see live.

You have to win a lottery to even get a chance to buy a ticket – and competition is stiff. People wait their whole lives to hear it in person and most never do.

There we were in Vienna on December 31st with the opportunity of a lifetime. It was worth it at any price.

We RAN back.

In my morning journal entry for that day I wrote that we might try to get tickets to the concert if they were not too expensive. When we got home that evening after the concert, we were giddy!! I scrawled across the whole journal page, "*IT WAS WORTH IT!!!*"

Make life worth it.

Try to recognize those once-in-a-lifetime opportunities and grab them! Knowing what you want and having it clearly fixed in your mind (and written, of course) gives you a heightened ability to recognize those moments.

Would like

Maybe write a best-case scenario

"Would like" is interchangeable with "it would be nice."

Maybe you would like to spend some time in nature. Maybe you would like to learn a language. Maybe it would be nice to have a new car.

Things in the "would like" category generally have nothing important riding on them. Often, they are not pressing matters. There is usually no rush to get them. More than likely, you feel completely assured of your success.

Conversely, sometimes things you "would like" are outrageous goals (my favorite!). They may be so far out of the realm of possibility that your mind does not even bother to create resistance (so they come to you easily).

Have you ever wanted something SO badly, but it seemed like it would never come? Yet in the middle of wanting that thing, has something else shown up that was not even a real consideration (but wonderful and welcome)?

It can feel like the universe is playing with you. Something you want so badly just never comes while other, maybe more extravagant, things materialize in your life easily and effortlessly.

The difference is that those things you want so badly have too much riding on them. The things you would like are lighter.

If your desire were a pony, how much weight could you put on it? Every ounce would slow it down.

Let me tell you about the planter...

We live in a 1950's era house. As with any older house, the "to do" list is always a mile long. Many things fall into the "have to" and "need" categories.

For about a year I had often wistfully wished (as in, "it would be nice") for a raised planter on the patio. It would both solve an issue and provide garden space. It was barely even on the list of things to do.

Then – like magic – it all came together in one weekend. Friends pitched in. Trucks were provided. Dirt was gifted by a neighbor who had just done landscaping. Suddenly, we had a perfect planter box.

It happened so fast! It happened so easily! It turned out exactly the way I envisioned. It happened that way because there was no resistance to the goal.

Chapter 5 recap:

In chapter 5 you discovered how do determine whether or not you need to write a best-case scenario for the items on your HOP. You learned to sort by "have to", "need", "want", or "would like."

Remember that you can also rate your stress level or level of desire on a scale of 1-10.

Here is another handy visual. It will help you to pull this all together:

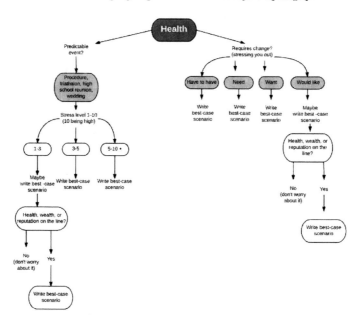

Here is an example of the process. You can use this for every category!

CHAPTER 6

Step 6

Develop Your Best-case Scenario

Now you have a comprehensive list of your upcoming predictable events, desired experiences, stressors, wants, and just about everything else. Take a deep breath and relax.

This is the fun part.

It is time to create the best-case scenarios for items on your HOP that require one. This is where you will spend your time tweaking and polishing. This is where you will develop a story about your desires and tune in to what you want.

Writing the best-case scenario is ART. Here's why…

"Yes, but…"

Often when you make a best-case scenario, it is followed immediately by a "yes, but…" Those "yes, buts" are a cocktail of past experiences, learning, other people's limitations, what culture has taught us, and the myriad of "shoulds" designed to keep us from stepping out and dreaming big.

If you want to live an extraordinary life, you have to dream big!

Let me tell you a little secret. "Yes, buts" are saboteurs.

They keep you from focusing on what you really want. They lead you to ask for what you think you *can* get or what you think you *should* get. They are almost always based on *old information* and *old experiences*.

Why settle?

The truth is, if you ask for what you *think you can get* or what you think you *should get* instead of what you want, you will never be satisfied. Settling is the ultimate lose-lose situation.

If you don't ask, the answer is always no!

There are a lot of reasons why you might have "yes, buts." You might have past experiences that may make you feel like you cannot have what you want. In fact, those experiences may stand guard between you and what you want.

You may have tried and failed (big time!). Feeling burned, you might be hesitant to try again. That is totally natural. It is expected.

But even if your embarrassing failure happened yesterday, you are different today. You are wiser today. Things are different today.

Still, it can be hard to argue with the "yes, but."

So don't argue.

Work around the "yes, buts."

Here is a way to write a best-case scenario that goes around the "yes, buts".

When you think about your goal, what do you focus on the most – the mechanics of *how* it will happen or *your purpose* for doing it? Your purpose will usually be at the top of your mind, but the *how* will often be what dominates your attention.

You may have heard the old saying that you might forget what someone says or does, but you will always remember *how they made you feel.*

Does thinking about your best-case scenario make you feel tired or defeated?

If so, you may be too focused on *how* it will all happen. It is human nature to get caught up in *how* you will do something and the logistics of it all. "Yes, buts" are almost always about the *how.*

"Yes, but...I have failed before..." (how)

"Yes, but...so-and-so will never change..." (how)

"Yes, but...I don't have the education/experience / status / connections / money..." (how)

Many "yes, buts" are a fear of failure based on your own past failure or on exposure to other people's failures.

Failure usually occurs in the implementation part of the plan. Therefore, it is almost always a *how* issue.

The purpose and goal may have been valid. However, the method or process used did not work as expected.

How often do things work out the way you think they will?

The *how* changes. It can be unpredictable in the most controlled circumstances. Things often happen differently than you expect them to.

You can almost never control the how!

Think about it. Ask NASA or any event planner. Even space launches, carefully monitored laboratory testing, and tightly planned events go awry.

What would happen if you focused on the outcome – the why?

Have you ever wanted something so badly that you simply had to have it? Can you remember a time when your purpose and reason were so compelling that you *made it happen*?

What got in your way then? Who showed up to support you? How long did it take you to get what you wanted? Probably not long!

That is what happens when you focus your attention and efforts on the *why*. You line up with your greater reason or purpose for wanting something.

Any *how* will work when you are aligned with the *why*. In fact, things often happen in extraordinary ways. Supporting elements come together for you. The right people show up. Resources are suddenly available.

When I wanted to go to law school, I put in applications to several schools. There was one I really wanted to attend in New Orleans. In fact, I wanted to go there so badly that I signed a lease and made a deposit on an apartment before I had been notified of acceptance.

Great apartments were scarce and expensive at the time. I knew exactly what I wanted.

There was no Plan B.

My family was shocked! They could not believe that I would take that leap of faith. But it was not a leap on faith alone. I was unwaveringly aligned with my goal and knew it would work out. It did.

I knew what I wanted. That helped me to recognize the opportunity when it arose. It also made me bold enough to seize the opportunity before it slipped away.

When you do not have a clear *why*, even the most thoughtful and well planned *how* will flounder. Without passion and congruence with what you want, things rarely work out well.

It might get done. But it will be tough going. When you look back on it, you may do so with a feeling of exhaustion.

When things come together for you, it feels like the planets align in your favor. The impossible becomes possible. When you look back it is with a feeling of accomplishment and exhilaration. You remember your time working toward your goal with fondness.

Aligning with your WHY creates congruence.

When you are congruent, your actions, thoughts, deeds, resources, and energy line up with your goal. You focus like a laser on the object of your desire.

Congruence with your goal is one of the most powerful feelings a person can ever experience. It allows you to wield astonishing influence.

Remarkable leaders throughout history have been congruent with their goal or purpose. Consider Joan of Arc, Martin Luther King, Jr., Mahatma Gandhi, or John Muir. They moved mountains and got things done. They were not so different from you!

You have experienced being congruent with your goals in the past. The HOP will help you gain consistent congruence with the goals you set in the future.

For everything on your big list of predictable events, upcoming experiences, stressors, "have to's", "needs", "wants" and "would like's", there is a *why*.

Line up with the WHY

In this part, you are going to line up with the *why* behind every important goal. That alignment is the fast track to making it a reality.

Here are the steps you will take to create your best-case scenario. This will help you to align with your desire, become congruent, and circumvent the "yes, buts."

Find the desire

Make it personal/subjective

Find the why – attach it to a feeling

Find the desire

What is your best-case scenario? Be honest and do your best to articulate what you really want and not what you expect or think you deserve. Sometimes they are the same. Many times they are not.

If your best-case scenario involves other people or circumstances changing, think about it only from your subjective point of view. How would *you feel* when/if they changed?

Carve that feeling out from the rest of the information and focus only on it. How would you feel differently than you feel now? Relieved? Respected? Free? Happy? Loved? Secure?

That feeling is your objective. If you can achieve that feeling, does it really matter how you get there?

By acknowledging your *why*, you open up many more possibilities for the *how* factor.

Imagine being all the way on the other side of having achieved your best-case scenario. Mentally try it on. Get into it as if you were living that moment. Imagine looking out of your own eyes.

What would it be like? Describe the emotions you would feel in that moment.

For example, say you have a ticket in coach for a very long flight. Maybe you have to go directly into work meetings upon arrival. Your best-case scenario might be to get upgraded to a better seat.

Why?

It would be more comfortable! You would have more leg room. You might even get better food, quiet, and have a chance of getting rest.

All of that is great, but *exactly* what would it do for you? How would you *feel* upon arrival?

You would feel more refreshed, well rested, in a better mood, and lucky (you got upgraded!). That lucky feeling might even translate to confidence. That extra confidence could help you to perform better in meetings upon your arrival.

Your true best-case scenario is to be alert, on your game, and perform well when you arrive.

I wonder...

If you have trouble imagining your best-case scenario, try using the statements, "I wonder...." or "What would happen if...?" When you phrase things this way, it adds the possibility of the unexpected. It reminds you that anything can happen.

Here are a few examples...

"I wonder how I would perform if I arrived well rested, refreshed, and in a good mood?"

"I wonder what it would be like if so-and-so and I got along and worked well together?"

"What if I felt proud of my body and confident in my clothes?"

"What would it be like if I loved going to work every day?"

When you pose questions to yourself in this way, it activates your brain to answer the question. Mentally ask your question and then leave some time for your mind to work on it. You may be surprised what comes up!

Chapter 6 recap:

In chapter 6 you discovered how to get around your "yes...buts" by focusing on your "why." You learned the power of congruence and of tuning into your goals.

Practice aligning with your purpose for having a goal.

Start examining the "why" behind the things that you do and the goals that you set. You will notice a pattern emerge that will help you to be more in line with your true overall purpose.

CHAPTER 7

Step 7

Craft a Juicy Story

Turn your best-case scenario into a juicy story.

You know how to focus on your best-case scenario by looking for the feeling behind what you want. Now, turn it into a story that you tell in the past tense.

Imagine that you are writing a letter to a good friend about how you successfully achieved your best-case scenario. This particular friend is a VIP and your best cheerleader.

Your friend will want to know all of the details about your achievements so they can share your success and happiness. You can also imagine writing a letter to yourself in the past.

I construct the letter like this:

Start where you are. Acknowledge how you feel or felt about the situation. What you feel is real!

Validate your feelings about the situation by describing them honestly. Doing this acts to establish a starting point and helps you get your bearings.

Move toward a better possibility. Loosen the reins a little bit. Open up to the possibility of new information, people, or circumstances that could change the situation.

This is the area of potential change. You cannot easily predict what that change might be. It is ok to put something here like, "My mindset changed," or "Something happened that changed everything."

Go for the goal. What do you want the outcome to be? Focus on how you will *feel* when you realize your ideal outcome.

The best way to teach you how to do this is to show you. Here are examples in each category that can help you to write your best-case scenario stories.

Health

Here is an example of creating a best-case scenario for a health stressor.

One of my clients injured his knee two weeks before an important trip. The trip had been planned for quite some time and involved several day-long walking excursions.

He was so worried that he would have to cancel or skip the walking tours! He could only focus on the worst-case scenario. We worked together to come up with an alternative scenario that relieved the stress and worry.

His best-case scenario was to enjoy seeing the sites. He wanted to somehow be able to take full advantage of the planned activities.

He wanted to have a good time and feel good while he was on this much-needed vacation. His story went like this:

We started where he was – *"I was so worried when I hurt my knee! It seemed like my vacation was already ruined. I was going to have to scrap all of my plans. I had been looking forward to this for so long. I was disappointed and frustrated."*

Then we moved toward a better possibility – *"I immediately decided to listen to my body and rest. I did everything possible to help my knee heal. My body heals like a champ. I gave it an opportunity to do that.*

Before long it got to a point where I felt pretty good. I thought about going back to normal activity but I waited a little longer. I continued to rest until a few days before my flight."

Then we went for the goal – *"The way I took care of my knee was perfect. By the time I arrived on vacation the injury was a non-issue.*

We had a wonderful time seeing the sights. I remembered to be kind to my body. Overall, it worked out extremely well. We had a great time, and my knee feels strong."

Notice the pattern?

We started where he was and validated his feelings of disappointment and anxiety. Only after acknowledging his feelings were we able to move into a better place of hope for his recovery. Once we worked through that, we were able to focus on the goal of him enjoying the scheduled activities in comfort.

The result? His knee was fully recovered for the trip. He reported being able to go on the walking tours with ease.

Want to be in better physical shape?

Here is an example that uses getting into better physical shape as a goal. There are plenty of reasons one might want to get into better physical shape.

The goal might be, "I want to lose weight" or, "I want to get into shape."

Goals like that are often met with resistance about *how* that might happen. Resistance can take the form of procrastination, distraction, "yes, buts," unrealistic or impossible diet and exercise plans, or fads that promise a quick fix.

The why

With just a *what* ("I want to get into better shape") and a *how* (dieting and/or exercise), you might not get very far. However, when you know the real *why* behind your desire to get into better shape, you will have a much easier time realizing your goal.

For example, if you ever want to see how fast someone can get into amazing shape, watch a bride prepare for her upcoming nuptials. Once the wedding date is set, there is only a certain amount of time to get in shape.

Weddings are sometimes the first time a bride-to-be is in the spotlight. It may be her first time as the focus of attention. That can be intimidating!

Brides want to shine on their wedding day. Google "bridal diet" and see how many results you get!

Most brides have a very clear *why* with a vision and a definite timeline. Nothing gets in the way of workouts and only the healthiest foods make it to the plate. It really is amazing to go through (oh yes, I did it) and to watch.

They buckle down and get phenomenal results. That is the kind of crystal clear focus that gets things done. You can have it, too.

It is all about using your imagination.

The bride has a clear vision of how she wants to look and feel on her wedding day. It is what she thinks about at the gym. It is what she is thinking about as she drifts off to sleep just a little bit hungry. It is what gets her out of bed for a ridiculously early run. It is why she turns down drinks with friends.

Her reason – her *why* – is powerful because her imagination gives it life. Your reason does not have to be groundbreaking or life changing, it just has to be *clear and imaginable*.

The bride's *why* is a short-term goal. Your goal for getting in shape will likely be a long-term goal. You probably want to make a sustainable lifestyle shift that will be easy to maintain and lead to better health and vitality.

Find the reason behind your best-case scenario. "I want to get into better shape so that…"

"My clothes will fit better and I will have more energy." That's OK but not very motivating, right?

"I can go on a 10-mile hike with my friends when they visit this summer." This is better but still a short-term goal.

"I can fully enjoy my entire life and be active, mobile, alert, and energetic no matter how old I get." This is much better and certainly long-term.

What is your *why*?

Imagine a time in the future when you are feeling vital, energetic, and healthy.

Feel the enthusiasm and confidence. Get into the vision and make it real in your mind.

Now write the story of how you got there, starting with today.

"Dear _____, (Remember, you are writing to that VIP friend!)

Start where you are – *"I was beginning to get really frustrated with my body. It wasn't cooperating! Worse still, I was not doing a very good job of supporting it. In my frustration, I would binge work-out and try short-term weight loss fads that were supposed to give me dramatic results."*

Move toward a better possibility – *"Then one day it occurred to me that I was treating my body in ways I would never treat a friend. My body supports me in the most amazing ways – despite what I do.*

I realized that if I supported my body the way it was supporting me, great health was within my reach. Moreover, my body WANTS to be healthy and is always healing and seeking that healthy equilibrium.

Once my mindset shifted, I got really clear about what it would be like and how it would feel to be at my peak health. I imagined what it would feel like to run up the stairs, dance, and wake up in the morning feeling good in my body.

It became about being the best me. My body has so much life and strength. I decided to support my body the best way I could – by treating it like a precious treasure. I made my body a priority."

Go for the goal – *"That shift in my thinking was more powerful than I could have imagined. The payoff was swift.*

Once I was clear about my goal, I naturally became more active. I walked more. I did more.

Some of the foods I had been eating lost their appeal. I began craving fresh, simple foods. My diet shifted without much fanfare

I felt better and more energetic. That inspired me.

Now I enjoy exercise. It fits into my day easily. Even though it can be challenging, it is always fun. I look forward to it.

So much of it just fell into place. It did not seem like work, but boy have I changed! I feel great! I look great! I love being in my body now!

This is a way of life that I can keep up. It is sustainable. It works. This is fun!"

What about day-to-day events?

Writing a best-case scenario for a lifestyle change like getting into shape is a big deal. The story needs to be carefully crafted. Take a quick look at a best-case scenario for a day-to-day event.

Always write a best-case scenario for things like going to the dentist, doctor, mechanic, or veterinarian. You want the people involved to be alert, rested, in a good mood, and on their game.

How you approach that situation can make all the difference. Your expectations and attitude are contagious!

Here is what an intention for the dentist or routine check-up might look like. This one can easily be adapted to many different situations. Use it as a template as you begin to create your own best-case scenarios for life.

"Dear _____,

Start where you are – *"I put off going to see _____ as long as I could. I had to go, but I was really nervous. What if I got bad news?? So many scary thoughts were running through my head. I had to make myself go."*

Move toward a better possibility – *"I talked to some friends. I got the emotional support I needed to make the appointment. I made my intention for the outcome. That made me feel more relaxed about going."*

Go for the goal – *"It turned out to be a lot easier than I expected. I felt comfortable and welcome. Amazingly, I was pretty relaxed the whole time.*

They did a fabulous job. I am glad I went. I feel good about going again when I need to."

Those are just examples of what you can do with your best-case scenario. Notice that everything is subjective?

Make it about you and *how you feel* as you work toward your goal. That is what your mind will use as a guide!

Wealth

Wealth can mean a lot of different things. However, stress related to wealth usually arises because of a deficit.

Since many people have some amount of stress related to either debt or not having enough wealth. We will use that as the best-case scenario for this category.

Often, a debt issue is really a not-enough-income issue. For now, change your thinking to focus on that instead.

The way to manage debt is to generate more income.

How? Maybe you have some ideas. Maybe you don't.

There may be ways to earn income that you have not considered or don't know. It may be very doable with the right information or a turn of circumstances.

If you get hung up on the *how*, you may lose focus on the *why*. Leave the *how* alone for now and focus on your *why*. When your purpose for earning more money is abundantly clear, you will open the door to financial abundance.

How will you be different when you have more than enough income? How will you feel? What will your life be like?

Can you imagine it?

Imagine having a positive cash flow with more money coming in than going out. Imagine the relief you will feel as more money flows into your bank account. Think about the feeling of pride, freedom, and control you will have.

What would you do if you had more than enough money? Would you give money to a charity? Would you develop your creativity through art or music? Would you travel?

Find your *why*. You are not on earth to struggle. You are here to experience, learn, and grow.

Maybe you are here to make a difference. Maybe you are here to support someone else while they make a difference. What will your difference or influence be?

Now begin thinking about your best-case scenario as if it has already happened. Imagine the feeling you will have as your bank accounts fill up and spill over into savings and investments.

Imagine that light feeling of being debt free. Imagine the feeling of power, knowing that you did it. Imagine the feeling of having control of your finances and knowing that *more is coming.*

Most importantly, how fun will your life be when your finances are a **source of joy**?

It might look something like this:

"Dear _____

Start where you are – *"I was so worried. For a while, it felt just hopeless, like I would never be able to earn enough to tip the scales and start building wealth. I was caught up in the process and in the struggle. I did not even know what my goals were anymore."*

Move toward a better possibility – *"And then something happened. I realized that I needed more information in order to increase my income. I began looking for resources that could help me discover new financial opportunities.*

I started thinking in terms of leaving a legacy. While I was mired down in the nuts and bolts of life, I had lost sight of my purpose. I wanted to reconnect with my reason for being here.

I'm not just along for the ride. I want to make a difference. Figuring out what that difference would be took some thought."

Go for the goal – *"But taking the time to tune into my greater purpose was so worth it. Once I had a clear goal, setting up benchmarks for meeting it was easy.*

Before, I had no goal, no direction. Once I had a clear goal, my direction became obvious.

As soon as I knew what I wanted, things started lining up for me. New opportunities appeared and I was ready for them.

I am already seeing real results. There has definitely been a shift. I feel blessed and enthusiastic about my finances.

The best thing is that I am enjoying it. Work used to leave me drained. Now it gives me energy. I look forward to it.

I always dreamed it could be like this. I feel so relaxed. I'm proud that things have worked out the way they have.

I did this. I never expected to have so much fun!"

On a smaller scale, you might be trying to keep costs in check on a project at home or at work.

Your best-case scenario might be to come in at or under budget.

"Dear _____,

Start where you are – *"I wasn't sure how we would be able to pull it off. Time was short and resources scarce."*

Move toward a better possibility – *"Then a few new pieces of information emerged that changed everything. With that, we were energized and able to come up with more creative solutions than the ones we had before."*

Go for the goal – *"Things suddenly made a lot more sense. Our new approach allowed us to do more with less. I was able to get into a good groove and do some great work all while staying alert to spending. We ended up working very well together. We came in within our budget at all times. I am already looking forward to the next project!"*

Relationships

Most people have at least one challenging relationship in their lives. Maybe it is a button pushing relative or a bully in the workplace. Maybe it is a needy friend.

Instead of focusing on that person changing, focus on how you want to feel when you are around them. Changing your perception of them and your reaction to them is a LOT easier than trying to change them!

How do you want the relationship to be in the future?

Think of the good relationships you have had over the years. How would you describe them? Maybe they were safe, loving, fun, relaxed, trusting, or supportive.

Think about the friends you click with the best, your favorite family members, and the people with whom you enjoy working. What, specifically, do you like about them? How do you feel about yourself when you are around them?

Use that information to decide how you want your relationships to be. Not all of your relationships will be perfect. However, you can make adjustments so that most of them are respectful, harmonious, and pleasant.

Here is a generalized best-case scenario to use for a challenging relationship:

"Dear _____,

Start where you are – *"I was feeling unloved and unappreciated. It seemed like every time I was around so-and-so, we ended up at odds. The tension always made me lose my cool. I would become cranky and combative. That is not how I want to be."*

Move toward a better possibility – *"Then something happened. Circumstances changed. There was a gradual shift in our relationship.*

I began to feel more comfortable and safe. I felt like myself around so-and-so and not as defensive or combative."

Go for the goal – *"I'm not sure who got it going, but I feel like we're both on the same team now. I feel confident in my interactions with him/her. I look forward to spending time with him/her now because I feel safe and respected."*

Here is another general story that you can use for a difficult relationship. I have used a work relationship in this example but you can change it to suit your unique situation.

"Dear _____,

Start where you are – *"It was getting to a point where I dreaded going to work. Everyone was so stressed out and negative all of the time. I really wasn't sure how much longer I could take it. I even started daydreaming about leaving."*

Move toward a better possibility – *"Then something shifted. I remembered all of the enjoyable things that made the job interesting to me in the first place. I decided to enjoy my day and be happy no matter what.*

I didn't make a big deal about it. I just quietly found ways to enjoy the day on my own.

When I made that decision, my focus changed. Like magic, my perception of the atmosphere at work changed, too."

Go for the goal – *"Maybe things were not as bad as I thought. Maybe my new mindset spread to the people around me. Whatever the case, I now enjoy going to work. It is easy for me to stay upbeat, optimistic, and positive.*

Better yet, this new mindset has also spilled over into my personal life. I am in a better mood most of the time. I handle stress much more easily now. Life is just a whole lot more pleasant!"

Adventure

Adventure can be anything from throwing a party to public speaking to travel. This category includes extraordinary events like those as well as the predictable events that punctuate the year.

If you think about it, the year has a way of naturally dividing into segments. School schedules, holidays, annual vacations, and events can provide a framework of yearly adventure. You may already divide your year into segments without even realizing it.

I divide my year up using the predictable events I look forward to the most. There are usually some changes but it is pretty predictable.

This structure helps me to set benchmarks in other areas. These events act as "treats" that I can look forward to when my goal benchmarks are met. Having something fun in my future inspires me to work toward my goals with extra enthusiasm.

Here is the adventure structure of my year:

New Year to Mardi Gras

Mardi Gras to Easter

Easter to our annual beach trip

Beach trip – to 4th of July

4th of July to Thanksgiving

Thanksgiving to Christmas

I add to that mix any other upcoming business or personal travel as well as any special events. Since many people travel during the year, I will use a travel example for this best-case scenario.

Ah Paris…

We went to France for a conference this past year. As we were preparing to leave, all sorts of things began happening in France. There were strikes, riots, protests, and floods. THE major European soccer event of the year coincided with the day of our arrival, adding the potential for delays and missed connections.

Our tickets were already purchased. Our hotels were already booked. We were already on the conference roster. Staying home was not an option.

In truth, we were worried! Seeing so much bad news can be alarming! It is always a great idea to write a best-case scenario for travel. When I start to worry, I know it needs to be a good one!

I carefully crafted my best-case scenario and included everything that came to mind.

"Dear___

Start where you are – *"We were starting to worry about our upcoming trip. It seemed like so much was going wrong at our destination. Safety was at the top of my mind. Would we be OK? Was it safe? Would the trains even be running? What if we got stuck?"*

Move toward a better possibility – *"While we were packing, I thought about places I had been before. Some of the places I visited (or lived) in the past were considered dangerous. Amazingly, I was always in the right place at the right time. I was always safe.*

It occurred to me that my big city alertness was deeply ingrained. It always guided my decisions about where to go and what to do.

Acknowledging that made me more relaxed about the trip. I started to daydream about how much fun we would have."

Go for the goal – *"Our trip to France was fabulous! We were comfortable on our flights. Travel went very well. We were always where we needed to be.*

We packed exactly the right things and were able to travel with just carry-on luggage. We were so proud of that!

Our hotels were perfect. We were happy with how clean they were. We loved the fabulous views. We both slept well the whole trip.

We met some wonderful people – including locals – and had some great nights out. We ate incredible French food.

This trip was definitely a networking success. We made some great contacts.

Paris was magical! It was beautiful. We saw so much in our short time there. I got some of the best photos. I can't wait to go back!

The dogs were so happy to see us when we got home! They were taken care of so well! I love that we have such a wonderful pet support system."

Now, let me tell you how it turned out…

To the airport on time…

We live about an hour and a half from the airport. Being smart travelers, we allotted enough time to get there with an hour to spare.

But things got busy. We dawdled and ended up with just enough time to get to the airport two hours before our international flight.

As we were getting close to the airport, a friend sent a text to me warning of an accident on the interstate. She said traffic was already backed up for miles. We missed that by just minutes!

We had good seats on the plane. Our seat neighbors on the flight were very pleasant and friendly. Our flight was one of the best international flights I have ever taken.

To the train on time...

We arrived in Paris with an hour and a half to make it to the train station (40 minutes away) to board our connecting train. Because of the soccer tournament, the line for customs was incredibly long. The zigzag of people was so long that we *could not even see* the customs windows.

When we were about seventy people away from the customs window, an agent arrived and let my husband, our seat mates, and me go to the front of the line. He gave us no explanation. That saved us about twenty minutes.

Because of the ongoing transportation strikes, the metro was not running. We opted for a taxi.

By the time we were in the taxi, we had thirty minutes to get to the train station – which was forty minutes away. Our driver was not hopeful.

Incredibly, there was very little traffic and our driver was determined. We arrived at the train station with about seven minutes to spare, paid the driver, ran to our train, and climbed aboard. The train took off as soon as we sat in our seats.

The conference...

The conference went exceptionally well. The presentation went perfectly. We both made fantastic business contacts. We had some fabulous nights out with new friends. It was a great trip!

Paris WAS magical! We saw more than we thought possible! I got amazing photographs. The night before we left, we happened to discover a brass band playing in a local club.

We were the only non-Parisians there. Everyone was welcoming and treated us like old friends. We felt like family. It was so much fun!

Going home...

We made it home safe and sound. The dogs were happy, healthy, and glad to see us.

What about events and things like that?

Parties happen! Events occur! They can be stressful.

If you are hosting an event or attending a function, it is always a good idea to write your best-case scenario. My best-case scenarios for social events usually include having interesting conversations, enjoying myself, and helping other people enjoy themselves. Afterward, I want to feel good about having attended.

When I am hosting an event I always want my guests to be there because they truly want to be there (and not out of duty or obligation). It is even better if the group of people who attend have a fun and lively chemistry with one another.

The first few times that I added those aspects to my best-case scenarios were strange. Some people who always showed up declined. Others went to heroic efforts to be there.

Time after time, this proved to be a good thing. Events got better and better throughout the years because the attendees were there to enjoy themselves.

Here is a short example of a party or event best-case scenario:

"Dear_____

Start where you are – *"I was worried about having everything just right for the event. There was so much to do! It was overwhelming! I also wondered if anyone would show up..."*

Move toward a better possibility – *"As things began to come together and the time drew near, I felt a weight lift. It felt good. I decided to enjoy myself and that was that."*

Go for the goal – *"The event went amazingly well. Everything worked out smoothly. The food was outstanding and there was enough of it.*

The clean-up was a breeze. We were able to get it done quickly without much effort.

Best of all, everyone we wanted to see was there! It was a wonderful combination of people. They mixed together thoroughly. Everyone was super social and people made new friends.

The right people showed up. The chemistry of the guests really made the night extra magical – what FUN!!!"

Surroundings

This category is for your life environment. Houses, cars, services, and things that shape your overall quality of life are found here.

You may not need to write many best-case scenarios in this category. I usually do it only when the situation involves a persistent problem, a potentially expensive issue, or a dangerous situation.

That pine tree…

One day I was checking the mail in our front yard. When I turned around to go back into the house, I noticed that one of our tallest, oldest pine trees was as dead as it could possibly be.

Worse, all of the limbs were on one side weighing the fall toward our roof. Even worse than that, the main trunk ran only a few feet from a power line *and* a metal roof.

You better believe we wrote a best-case scenario for that one! I held my breath every time the wind blew!

Here is what I wrote:

"Dear ____

Start where you are – *"The dead tree made me so nervous! It could not have been in a more dangerous place. It was leaning right toward the house."*

Move toward a better possibility – *"I got a referral for a tree trimmer. I liked him immediately."*

Go for the goal – *"We were so relieved that the tree trimmer was able to come so soon to remove the pine tree. Even better, he did it for a reasonable price. They did a fantastic and safe job removing the tree.*

They were in and out quickly and cleaned up the debris before they left. You would have never guessed that they had even been there!"

Here is what happened…

I contacted several tree trimmers. I finally got a name from a friend. Choosing him was easy – he was the only one who called me back.

We made a deal for the amount and it was extremely fair. However, because of their schedule and weather, the date for tree removal was up in the air. We did not know when to expect them to arrive.

We had guests visiting the following week. Though it was not included in the written best-case scenario, we wanted the tree gone before their visit.

The tree trimmers showed up early on the morning of the day our friends were set to arrive. They were lightning fast!

It was amazing how much got done in so little time. By noon they were rolling out, taking all of the debris with them.

They even cleaned up the lawn and blew the debris off of our driveway. You could not tell they had been there at all (except the tree was gone!). In fact, the yard looked better than usual!

Our friends arrived about an hour after the tree trimmers left.

Chapter 7 recap:

In chapter 7 you discovered how to create a story to accompany your best-case scenario. Practice writing best-case scenarios for the little things in life that you want. That will help you tune in to your own writing style.

Written correctly, your best-case scenario will uplift you. It will put a smile on your face and draw you forward toward your desired outcome.

Here is another handy visual – a mind map to help you envision the different categories of your life.

CHAPTER 8

Step 8

Make a Vision Board

Having your best-case scenarios written down is really all you need. In fact, I have scrawled them on the backs of receipts, jotted them down on Post-it notes, and emailed them to myself. That is enough. It works.

Want to make it even better?

Add images to your best-case scenarios of the future! When you add imagery, it turns your master document into an interactive vision board.

As you sort through your best-case scenarios, create a master document. It can be in a scrapbook, a journal, or on your computer.

I create mine on the computer because it allows me to access it easily to make adjustments. It also creates an accessible record through the years.

Start by adding pictures to your best-case scenarios.

If you want to feel strong and energetic enough to go mountain climbing, put a photo of healthy mountain climbers next to your best-case scenario for health.

Want to have a better relationship with your family? Insert a happy photo of you all together next to your best-case scenario for family relationships.

Want a new car? Insert a photo of you smiling next to your ideal car (even a picture of it will work).

Create a scrapbook of the things you want to have in your life. The more you bring it to life on the pages of your scrapbook or on your vision board, the more likely you will bring it into your real life.

You get the idea. Play with it!

Chapter 8 recap:

In chapter 8 you discovered how to add an element of fun and effectiveness to your Hands On Plan by adding imagery.

Add photographs, videos, and anything else that you think would bring your Hands On Plan to life. Enjoy the process!

CHAPTER 9

Step 9

Tap into Your Ideal Future

This is the final and most powerful part of the whole process. Just like you tapped in everything that went well last year, tap in your upcoming best-case scenarios.

It is an easy step that will almost always lead to adjustments and changes to your best-case scenarios. It also calls for some attention to feelings on your part.

If, when you tap through a best-case scenario, you feel lighter, happier, and enthusiastic, it is a good one. The better it feels, the better it works.

If you feel detached, uninterested, silly (or worse), it is not a good best-case scenario for you. Take a quick look back at some of the examples in chapter 7 and modify your story until it feels good.

Check and make sure that your best-case scenario is truly subjective and written about the way *you* feel or want to feel. Make sure your best-case scenario is written about what you really want and not what you think you should have or expect.

Your story is about your feelings and what you want, even if it is outlandish. Be true to that. Re-write your story until you can tap through it and feel good.

When you can't write the story...

There is a chance that you will run into situations or desires for which it is difficult to create a best-case scenario. Again, this process can help you to identify areas where you might need to perform deeper emotional work – perhaps with a coach or therapist.

There are occasions when hurt, regret, anger, or other negative emotions are so strong that they hide the *why* from you. When that happens (and if you have some juicy goals, it might), take that as your cue to find a coach, like me, who can help you to manage the emotions coming up around your goal.

How many times should you tap through your best-case scenarios?

Go through your best-case scenarios and tap them in as many times as feels good to you. Sometimes you will just feel it click into place. It will feel complete.

Sometimes it takes a little longer to line up with your desire. Keep Tapping until you feel a shift.

Your mind may begin to wander while you are Tapping through your best-case scenario. It might begin to feel like you are just going through the motions. Those are clues that you have probably tapped through it enough.

Remember, your HOP is a living document. It is not only ok to make adjustments, it is necessary. Change it if the situation, timeline, or people involved change.

Remember to have fun with this process! You can go through the whole thing at once if you have the time. If not, focus on one category at a time and work through them systematically.

Join the conversation at www.nancytiltonhand.com. Sign up for my updates and stay in the loop about how I am using this process. You will find the answers questions you might have about successfully using this system on a daily basis.

I look forward to hearing from you and sharing your stories of success!

Nancy

PS –

Dear Reader,

Just when I thought the Hands On Plan was finished, something happened that showed me just how powerful this process can be.

I recently returned from a journey that tested MY Hands On Plan in a way I could never have imagined. It shows how the plan is always a working plan and that *it will work even if you don't work it.*

Below is the story of Vienna and hearts – of doubt and trust.

Last December, my husband asked me if I wanted to go to Vienna. Well, duh! No brainer. It is one of my favorite places! He did not say anything more about it until February.

That is when I found out that he had been accepted to present at a very important industry conference. The best part? His airfare and accommodations were covered by work.

We decided to make the most of it and planned a 17-day trip that started in Budapest and ended in Munich. Of course, we worked out our HOP right away.

Our HOP included easy travel, great networking, beautiful weather, seeing and experiencing everything we wanted to, magic moments, healthy/happy dogs when we got home…the usual.

From the moment we booked tickets, everything went smoothly.

My husband ended up presenting his research at several other conferences over the summer. It was WAY more travel than we anticipated back in December. I joined him when possible but saved most of my travel for the big trip to Vienna.

A few weeks before our departure for the Vienna trip, my brother was diagnosed with a heart condition and scheduled for surgery. From that moment on, I went into a frantic, emotional tug-of-war.

How could I leave him? I felt like a jerk even thinking about it.

I had absolutely no doubt in my brother's strength and overall health. I knew that he would be fine. His partner was incredibly loving and supportive.

Because it was not an emergency, they were able to plan his surgery and recovery in advance down to the last detail. They had things under control and then some. His team was stellar.

He wrote his own HOP. His best-case scenario was clearly laid out. Once he had done that, I felt a little bit better. However, I was still on the fence about the trip.

Two nights before our flight, I was pretty much packed. The bags were ready.

Then I freaked out and unpacked. Everything went back into drawers and closets. I still couldn't decide what to do.

I began to doubt this process and my HOP. How could I possibly put out a book about a system that was unreliable?

Then it occurred to me that my brother had an HOP for his procedure and for his recovery (which, by the way, is going perfectly!). We had a plan for our trip that had long been in place. By staying, I might have disrupted *his* plan.

I repacked my bags and decided to go. I made arrangements to be available by phone at all times.

But I was still on the fence. I really, truly wanted to be in two places at once. I felt guilty for leaving.

Out-of-sync with our HOP

We had a great trip! It really was wonderful. It was magical. Things went smoothly.

However, it would have been more enjoyable if we had taken time on the front end to realign with our HOP before embarking. The stage was set for the trip; we just weren't ready to go on it. Something was off.

The emotional impact of a family crisis coupled with the alarm of a natural disaster (in my hometown) was enough to put us *out of sync with our HOP*. The thing is, none of the issues that made me feel so emotional had anything to do with the trip we had planned.

Have you ever seen a cartoon of a horse finishing a horse race while the jockey rides backward in the saddle?

That was our Vienna trip. The HOP for our trip was in place and it worked out perfectly. It finished the race.

It crossed the finish line beautifully – with us hanging on and flopping around a little bit. If we had been more aligned with our HOP, we would have ridden it to first place. It would have been a glorious ride!

It was still a fantastic trip. The weather was perfect for us for 17 days (in three different countries). The networking was stellar for both of us, travel was delightful (planes arriving ahead of schedule, super easy customs, short lines…), and it was magical.

We got to see the things we wanted to see and eat what we wanted to eat. We made new friends and reacquainted with friends from the past.

IT, the trip story, was written and played out as planned. It was good to go. We were thrown off by emotions that were unrelated to our HOP. That made an impact on the *tone* of our trip.

Next time, we will take time to re-align with our HOP and balance to it.

Re-align

The message is that your plan is *your plan*. Before you get sidelined by other things and events outside of your purview, check to see if they are part of your plan.

If not, take some time to balance back into your plan. Re-align with it so that you can ride it to a first-place finish.

Happy Planning,

Nancy

Here is a quick recap of the steps:

Appreciate

Tap into success

Decide what you want

Decide what needs a best case scenario

Develop best-case scenario

Craft a juicy story

Make a vision board

Tap it in

Nancy Tilton Hand, JD, NLP Trainer

Author Trainer Coach

Learn Faster. Communicate Better. Negotiate More Effectively.

Nancy Tilton Hand, JD is an executive coach, author, and corporate trainer. She helps professionals manage information efficiently, communicate effectively, and negotiate successfully.

Her first book, *"Beyond Rainmaking: Accelerated Learning Techniques for Law School, The Bar Exam, and Beyond,"* contains the secrets to successfully managing massive amounts of information. It is the result of over 30 years of research and her own experience overcoming the effects of ADD and dyslexia.

She draws on her personal expertise, scientific research, and real-life experiences to create compelling and easy-to-understand presentations. She is an energetic presenter whose words resonate with the new generation of professionals seeking a competitive advantage in today's workforce.

"Beyond Rainmaking: Accelerated Learning Techniques for Law School, The Bar Exam, and Beyond" – ISBN: 978-0983727675 – is available at major booksellers. Beyond Rainmaking contains techniques that can be used by people of any profession to improve performance.

Interested in how Nancy uses this information? Check out her blog at www.nancytiltonhand.com.

Contact Information:

Nancy Tilton Hand, JD, NLP Trainer

P.O. Box 3154 Auburn, AL 36831

Email: nancy@nancytiltonhand.com

Author Website: www.nancytiltonhand.com

Appendix A

According to my findings, Tapping is the powerful combination of several, very effective, highly documented, psychological tools. Combined, they are an incredibly potent combination.

Most importantly, *you can use it on your own* as a fast, easy-to-use behavior and mindset change tool.

Here are some of the reasons Tapping works so well:

Intention – written and verbal

Tapping creates an intention for change.

We have already talked about why having a written intention – a best-case scenario – works so well. Knowing what you want points you toward your desired outcome. It changes your attitude and behavior to support your goal.

Your intention is powerful! Any time you use Tapping, whether it is for stress relief or peak performance, you will do it for a reason.

That reason is your *intention for change*. It will guide you toward a better outcome.

This process can be improved by saying your intention *out loud* as you tap. When you do, you declare your best-case scenario.

That declaration adds fuel to the process. Psychologically, daring to say what you want (out loud!) has a huge impact.

It activates the part of human nature that makes you stand behind the things you say. It makes you more likely to follow through.

You probably know that it can be helpful to talk about problems with a friend or family member. Doing so can help you gain a different perspective and devise solutions to problems.

In fact, talk therapy is one of the most widely used behavioral change modalities. Trained professionals and clergy are often employed when subject matter is too delicate, personal, or revealing to discuss with close friends or family.

Studies show us that social relationships affect health and shape health outcomes throughout life. They have a cumulative impact on health as years go by. Having friends to talk to might be one of the reasons relationships are so important for your health.[4]

You can also talk to yourself and achieve similar therapeutic results.

Recent studies show that talking aloud to yourself can help you to better adapt to stress and manage your emotional response to it. Therefore, Tapping while talking aloud about your challenges and stressors allows you to directly benefit from that stress relief response. You can also use this method to amplify and turbocharge the emotions connected to your wins and successes.[5]

Soothing through touch

Have you ever held someone's hand when you were scared?

Have you ever really needed a hug after a tough day?

Human touch is an incredibly effective way of calming someone in times of stress. We rock crying babies. We hug people when they have had a hard day.

Have you ever noticed how often people touch their faces when they are scared, tense, upset, or having difficulty making a decision? Do a Google image search for any of those emotions and you will discover an abundance of hand-to-face imagery! Maybe we are hardwired to tap.

The research supporting soothing through touch is well established. Much of it involves the effect of soothing touch on the amygdala – the part of your brain responsible for the fight or flight response.

Skin to skin contact is calming. Contact between a mother and newborn child has been shown to help the baby stay calm and sleep better. It also enhances and regulates the development of the baby's brain.

The healing power of touch is not just for babies! Skin to skin contact is an important emotional regulator throughout life. It can lower stress hormone levels (like cortisol) and raise "feel good" hormone levels (like testosterone and oxytocin).[6]

Even better, the stress busting, brain building, feel-good-hormone-generating power of touch does not have to come from somebody else.

New research shows us that it that you can generate it on your own. You can get stress relief and a rise in oxytocin by using self-soothing touch. So go ahead, touch yourself!

Hugs are healthy. Give yourself one now! Reach around and pat yourself on the back or clap!

The results might even be better if you do it on your own. Treating yourself and your body with love and appreciation is powerful!

One study revealed that people who treat themselves well in times of stress are healthier and recover from traumatic experiences more quickly.[7] Another found that the anti-stress effects of oxytocin are extra potent when oxytocin is released in response to low intensity touch stimulation.[8]

Does Tapping fit that bill? You bet!

Raises oxytocin and testosterone levels

Tapping calms the amygdala and helps reduce stress response by raising oxytocin and testosterone levels. This helps you to feel better and think more clearly.

Oxytocin is amazing in many ways. It is a highly effective pain reliever with powerful analgesic, anxiety inhibiting, and antidepressant effects.[9]

Testosterone makes you feel powerful, motivated, and resourceful. It is important for spatial reasoning, clear thinking, and decision-making. It is your oomph hormone.

Lowers cortisol levels

Tapping can also cause a decrease in cortisol levels. High cortisol levels are associated with stress and the fight or flight response. When cortisol goes up, testosterone goes down and vice versa.[10] That is why it is difficult to reason and be creative when you are tense or panicky.

Tapping puts you back in control of your emotions. How is that for taking your health into your own hands?

Reconsolidation

For memories, Tapping works in concert with a process called reconsolidation. Reconsolidation is the term researchers at New York University use to describe what happens when we recall memories.

Researchers found that each time a study participant recalled a memory, the memory was vulnerable and susceptible to change for a short period of time. After that, the memory was reconsolidated or recommitted, to long-term memory.

This retrieval and reconsolidation process can be interrupted. New information can be added or taken away. When it is reconsolidated and re-filed in long-term memory, the memory is *forever changed.*

Researchers found that when new information was added or old information was changed, participants noted differences in both their recollection of the memory and the behaviors associated with it.[11]

Have you ever had a memory of an experience change radically after you received new information about it?

Maybe you ended a relationship with someone and all of the memories that were great before became suddenly...different. When the new information is added, it alters memories in a fundamental way.

In the case of a bad memory, you can add or alter the memory to diffuse negative emotions associated with it. In the case of a great memory, you add emphasis to make the emotions associated with it stronger and more ingrained.

Tapping adds new information that can lessen the impact of negative emotions on your behavior and your mindset.

For example, someone with a public speaking fear might want to tap while recalling negative past experiences related to speaking out or being the center of attention.

Because Tapping increases the flow of feel-good hormones, it can also amplify the effects of past positive experiences.

For example, someone about to take an exam may want to tap while recalling their most positive test-taking experiences. Someone competing in a sport might want to review past accomplishments and wins.

When you tap, you are adding a wealth of information to any memory or circumstance that may have caused you to tap. You are adding touch information. If you are talking through it out loud, you are adding auditory information. You also add kinesthetic information through the vibration in your throat, the movement of your mouth, and your breath.

Finally, those magic "Meridians"

There may actually be something to them…

More and more research is pointing to the idea that certain acupuncture points correspond with areas of dense nerve collection. That may make those particular meridian points more effective places to tap. Researchers at Georgetown University found that acupuncture points in the stomachs of test rats affected the same mechanisms used by some common antidepressants and anti-anxiety drugs.[12]

What does it all mean?

It means that Tapping is a powerful combination of several tried-and-true, scientifically supported methods of emotional and behavioral management.

Used together, this dynamic combination allows you to change your attitude, habits, behaviors, and mindset more easily.

The power is in your hands.

Notes

1. Matthews, Gail. "Goals Research Summary." *Dominican University* (2013).

2. Stephen, Andrew T., and Michel Tuan Pham. "On feelings as a heuristic for making offers in ultimatum negotiations." *Psychological Science* 19.10 (2008): 1051-1058.

3. Matthews, Gail. "Goals Research Summary." *Dominican University* (2013).

4. Umberson, Debra, and Jennifer Karas Montez. "Social relationships and health a flashpoint for health policy." *Journal of health and social behavior* 51.1 suppl (2010): S54-S66.

5. Lepore, Stephen J., Jennifer D. Ragan, and Scott Jones. "Talking facilitates cognitive–emotional processes of adaptation to an acute stressor." *Journal of personality and social psychology* 78.3 (2000): 499.

6. Raylene Phillips, M. D. "The Sacred Hour: Uninterrupted Skin-to-Skin Contact Immediately After Birth." *Newborn & Infant Nursing Reviews* 13 (2013): 67-72.

7. Leary, Mark R., et al. "Self-Compassion and Reactions to Unpleasant Self-Relevant Events: The Implications of Treating Oneself Kindly." *Journal of Personality and Social Psychology* 92.5 (2007): 887-904.

8. Uvnäs-Moberg, Kerstin, Linda Handlin, and Maria Petersson. "Self-soothing behaviors with particular reference to oxytocin release induced by non-noxious sensory stimulation." *Frontiers in psychology* 5 (2015): 1529.

9. R Goodin, Burel, Timothy J Ness, and Meredith T Robbins. "Oxytocin-A Multifunctional Analgesic for Chronic Deep Tissue Pain." *Current pharmaceutical design* 21.7 (2015): 906-913.

10. Mehta, Pranjal H., and Robert A. Josephs. "Testosterone and cortisol jointly regulate dominance: Evidence for a dual-hormone hypothesis." *Hormones and Behavior* 58 (2010): 898-906.

11. Monfils, Marie-H., et al. "Extinction-reconsolidation boundaries: key to persistent attenuation of fear memories." *Science (New York, NY)* 324.5929 (2009): 951.

12. Eshkevari, Ladan, Eva Permaul, and Susan E. Mulroney. "Acupuncture blocks cold stress-induced increases in the hypothalamus–pituitary–adrenal axis in the rat." *Journal of Endocrinology* 217 (2013): 1-10.

CPSIA information can be obtained
at www.ICGtesting.com
Printed in the USA
FFOW01n0909290418
46378773-48086FF